for KT, from overseas

a collection of poems by
Benjamin Richard Nicoll

**TIRED COAST
PUBLISHING** ™

for KT, from overseas

TIRED COAST PUBLISHING
San Diego, California

Library of Congress Catalog Card Number:
ISBN: 978-0-692-16448-8

Printed in the United States of America

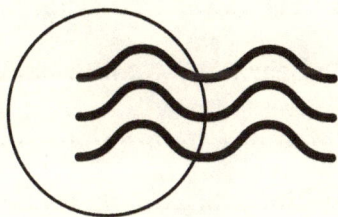

for KT, from overseas

I Will Guide You

Not the biggest biceps,
or sense of direction like Magellan,
but I have a light, a beard,
and now, I have met you.

You, have a few skills I could use,
so, you will guide me, too.
No, not royalty like King Arthur,
nor a noggin like Einstein.
No, don't give out gifts like St. Nick.
But, KT,
people will pay good money
for this suit of mine,
and I will sell it, for you and I.

My friend Harold, said he saw you fishing.
Fish are good for me; they contain omega-3.
I am deficient of this third omega.
Omega-3 gives my beard an honorable shine,
enlightens my senses, makes me skip, makes me smile,
acts as fuel, when we need a fire.

We must take off, tonight.
Pack a fishing pole, a canvas, a sing-along song;
I will find a red hat for you so you fit in for a while.
I can't offer you much, KT,
for I am a mere gnome with a minute stature,
but I was given a hand I will share,
a laughter that can tame a bear,
and a heart that closely resembles a compass.

And I have learned from the good old gnomes from
past that a friend can do more for your soul than a
pocketful of gold.
KT, just wait and see, how tall we become at the place
I shall guide thee.

Together, we will prance, on a mossy painted path,
to a land of the gnomes, called breeze block.
It is a cul-de-sac made of sea-green colored grass.
There are boomboxes lined up playing hillbilly banjo
tunes.

I swear, everyone floats around on stilts,
holding back smirks.
You will awaken to all the small amazing things
happening in life,
that are so easy to overlook.
Like a beetle in the bark,
the thread in a loved one's scarf,
or the tingling feeling felt deep in your bones,
when in unity with a million other small singing souls.

KT, we will dance all bright-eyed and bushy-tailed.
All the wildflowers will be at nose height,
so we can revel in their magical scented delight.
Our heads will be held high
towards the infinite sky,
because all the unkind things
will be left below our knees.

And when the moonlight spreads across this elf land,
everything will feel just right.

But, promise me,
you will help guide me,
and I promise,
I will help guide you
to this special place.

And when we return,
if we ever decide to return,
this memory will be kept in a secret spot in our pocket.
We will plant ourselves stoically in the front lawn,
and when the common people ask where we went,
we, just, we won't respond.

Darling

I don't want to wake up
among the empty cans,
the one-night stands,
among the sinners, darling.

I want to wake up to baby's breath,
a warm cuppa tea,
a view of wild wheat
blowing towards the sea.

Dreaming of New Jersey

Bruce Springsteen,
a tin of gin.
Turn it up for the Americans.

Like the belly of a teenage boy
on a first date/dance
in the dark
barefoot under a boardwalk
by the sea,
the smell of fireworks
and fragility.

Johnny Rockets,
a splash of Coke.
Someone just spit on my
Levi's coat.

No one knows the taste of a burger;
the states just chew, chew, chew
on nothing at all.

No more dining room tables,
nor prayers for all sentient beings.
It's all couch and "reality" T.V.

No more substance,
that's why my grandparents use so much salt.
No more idols,
rest in peace, T.P.

God bless Bruce,
those who admit fragility,
those who sit by the fire
and dance around the debris,
like me.

Lake Prank

It's a few friends by the lake,
truck reversed in,
tailgate down,
smiles all around.

Pelly, he never fishes,
he'd rather swim and sing,
float with his belly down,
dream about mangos and wedding rings.

KT sits cross-legged,
loves the stillness of the line,
finds some sort of metaphor in it,
for the divine.

She watches Pelly ponder in the pond,
bites her nails to stay sane.
She hooks a large something,
spits out a cherry-colored nail,
runs to the shoreline,
and reels in with no care.

She thinks it will be dinner,
a large trout, maybe bass,
turns out Pelly tied his boot to the line,
he grins, while KT isn't jazzed.

Racecar Visa

Long-distance love.
Saltwater, grit, nostalgia.
Tears, tears, tears,
to fill a lake,
all written,
for you.

Visa racecar, racecar visa,
I have termed this portion,
of life.
Life of,
Pelly.

A feather from the limb,
never to be read again.

Amazing,
how I went back,
and you came coastal
like palindrome.

A box of belongings,
buried atop a bluff.

Racecar,
was my mind,
you were the pace car,
going back, going forth,
like boomerang.

I tried Zen,
listened to self-help.
Indy 500, checkered flags,
waving, crashing.

Visa,
some purchase goods.
For me,
visa, in the way of the one I love.

Like palindrome,
like racecars, like boomerang.
Waiting for visas
drove me mad.

Goddamn,
racecar visa.

I Am the Bear

There is no reason to worry
for I am the bear, the bird, the banjo,
the paws, the wings, the strings.

When I breathe in;
I am the bear -
powerful.

When I breathe out;
I am the bird -
weightless.

When I listen;
I am the banjo -
present.

When I play these strings
I recall the air between
that felt so stricken
when we last met.

Then,
I recall Alexander Supertramp,
"How important it is in life
not necessarily to be strong,
but to feel strong."

Big Sur

One day I will live in a cabin by the sea
nestled in the woods of Big Sur, CA.
No one will know I'm there;
except for a few squirrels, blue jays, and the mailman.
Eat kelp on the deck, sip on foreign teas,
with my nice, warm flannel on.
There will be a telescope, record player,
and the infinite sea
to keep me company.

I'll write spontaneous prose,
like my heroes Kerouac, Cassady, and Burroughs.
Drink coffee and eat my veggies.
Walk to work every day
to my self-started deli, *The Big Surve*.

Come visit me, dear friends;
we'll skip stones,
sing songs,
take deep breaths,
catch the pine tree breeze,
and stare at our knees
while swaying off Bixby Bridge.

I don't want fortune or fame,
that would drive me insane.
I can barely handle anonymity.
Couldn't imagine people knowing my name,
and defeat the reason for hiding on Redwood Lane.

Teenage Riot

Back then,
I felt so at ease,
carved our names into trees,
walked next to ocean breeze.

Back then,
we fell into a bliss-filled daze,
with butterflies haloing our heads
next to the river's edge.

The wind,
just right for kites back then.
Remember, we would see how high we could get?
We were a teenage riot,
back then.

An Homage to Adolescence

Our friendship,
like a playlist of old road-trip rock songs.

Bombing Avenida Calafia one morning;
early, July '04.
Dirt roads with a Hobie plank beneath our feet.
Rusty trucks, rubber wheels,
led us to the waves that day.

First beer in the woods.
Observing those fragile deer.
Snowy roads with a sled under our ass.
Older boys driving trucks,
tossing ski ropes into our hands,
led us to adolescence.

Now, it's morning and we are getting married.
Roosters alarm, early.
Hand in hand, always.
We pay those checks, daily.

Authentic and perfectly smooth,
we'll sit in rocking chairs
with our beautiful wives.
A view of memories
and maybe some sprouts in sight.

Singing those old,
road-trip rock songs.

Sunday Company

I am awake and it's morning.
Stepped foot on cement not far from the main room.
Could see my breath mixing with the coffee steam
like sugar with cream.

Now I sit, just Buddha mind and ceramic;
observing last night's dreams
and a few other,
beautiful things.

I am awake and it is a bit later.
The newspaper is good company.
It says the sun will shine on Monday.
It says the sun will shine on me today.

Although, my idols are underground,
and, you overseas.
It reminds me,
I am in good company.

ALOHA65

I stuck my arm out the window this morning
and gave a thumbs-up the size of a redwood to a
gentleman I don't know.

His vanity plate read ALOHA65,
a tattered California flag rested on his back seat,
a bouquet of wildflowers on the front,
and a boombox with too much bass roared
Tom Petty's, "Time To Move On."

The old man had to have been pushing 70, 80 or 90
miles per hour.
Authentic beard and a secondhand jacket,
he embodied rad.

But rad is not in his vocabulary;
the appropriate adjective would be bitchin'.
But this man doesn't care for adjectives,
for he's all verb.

When I Ran into You at the Turtle Pond in September at State;

I was a little drunk, or hungover,
guaranteed sad.

My head hanging like a leaf from a tree,
you said, "Chin up, buckwheat."

Buckwheat

I misplaced
my megaphone;
no substance in the words I say these days,
lofty loaf of white bread murmurs.

Time to slap some jam on buckwheat,
put on my chucks and a hard hat.
Dust the dirt from my knees,
floss my teeth,
sharpen the arrowhead,
rally the platoon,
hit the pavement,
by noon.

Oh no,
I misplaced
my megaphone;
the score went silent
for about a second.
The lights in the cinema
will return.
I apologize, my friends, for the inconvenience.
Eat your popcorn 'til my cinema returns.

My Mona Lisa

I write poems in my head,
and forget them by the time I go to bed.

I see movies in my dreams,
and forget them by the time the sun beams.

I paint a picture of Mona Lisa's sister,
instead of bristles, I use my whistle.

She floats in the air,
and my whistle keeps her there.

Red Datsun, Carma

I was sad,
so I visualized riding in my dad's old 'n' rusty,
red Datsun.
Under oak trees in Orange County,
radio playing Neil Young's,
"The Needle and the Damage Done,"
my young toes too short to
touch the ground.

He called her *Carma*.
I miss her,
like I miss you.

Open Letter

Said hi to the postman,
recited a poem.

Went on a run,
got the endorphins up.

Flip of the switch,
mind outta the ditch.

Grandpa, Holyday Hill High School

So I took some time off,
rested my head and popped some pills.
Rode my bike over the hills and far away,
as Zeppelin would say.
Towards my
expiration date.

I lay my face down,
 on my grandfather's grave,
"How was your day, John?"
I would say.
"Were you like me? Did you struggle with depression?
 Treat it with tobacco and meditation?
And do you find peace when you die?"

He avoided the question.
"Thanks for the bouquet,"
 he would say.
"Keep the album of mine in mind,
 read the books by our idols,
 and keep the sprouts in check,
 Pelly."

A slight bow,
 to grandpa, children, all sentient beings.
To a new found education.
"Thanks for guiding me," I would say.
And I was on my way,
 over the hills and far away.

You, Me and the Debris

Her words hit me,
like an arrow
splitting the apple
atop a head.

Her words hit me,
every syllable,
every well-constructed consonant
cut me in half.

Her words hurt me.
As I lay crumbled,
she
walked off.
She's
strong.
While I, underneath this skin,
all my emotions ever do is look for a reason to be frail.
It's very un-male like, or so they say, for a modern
man.
But it's who I am.

And that arrow of hers,
went straight through my skin that day.

I lay in the grass, corpse pose.
Observing my breath.
With the most un-stoic demeanor,
wishing I could be half as brave as her.

One day, I will learn how to shoot an arrow,
but for now,
I will lay in the grass collecting the other half of me,
the debris.

Chariots of Fire

Just breathe,
sip your coffee, stay sane,
hold my hardened hand.
You are my chariot,
I am your fire.
Look, my eyes,
just breathe.

Just see,
the color of nature,
all the subtleties in the sand.
You are my rock,
I am your roll.
Look, my eyes,
just see.

Now,
crop the bad parts from mind,
that you see and breathe.
Like drugs,
like global warming,
like death.

Then,
sneak out the back door,
to rolling hills.
Photoshop,
the good parts from mind.
Like daisies,
like Frisbees,
like blue jays.

We breathe, we see,
positively.
We breathe, we see,
fragility.

Fragile

You can be fragile, Pelly,
but we can't afford
for you to break.

Tie your love in a knot
and pretend like you're not hurt.
Even if you're a bundle of rage,
keep a smile on your face.

My therapist talks to herself while handing me pills,
with an expiration over the hills.
All I want is fresh air, a warm hug,
and a stream of tea.

I don't know if you understand me, Doc,
men aren't supposed to show their
fragility.

Painting Scenes of Our In-betweens

We would sing in tune, all afternoon.
Head to the shore, watch the tide return.
Question Jesus, question our parents,
all while enjoying the moment
without even knowing it.

We went looking for arrowheads,
four-leaf clovers in the hills behind Harry's house.
All we found was a rabbit, a Colt 45.
You made a friendship bracelet for me,
I collected seashells for you.
We were friends,
we were best friends.

Then we grew old,
not so very old,
just 23 years old.
You went to the Sunshine Coast,
and I stayed here with my parents
painting scenes of our in-betweens.

Space Miners

There's a miniature horse,
and a 2x4 piece of wood
in the mail for you.

I put the flag up,
the mailman that knows my name will understand.
We have a lot of work to do,
mate.

I heard there is gold on the moon,
pack that flannel
and flask.

I will guide you,
and figure out the rest.

Let's Take a Break from Our Afternoon Tea to Talk about a Subject Dear to You and Me

Let's talk about something,
the Suez Canal?
The Velvet Underground?
Siamese twins?
Or your acid trip in the sixties?

Something simple,
something complex,
or something that made you cry more than once.

Let's be fragile,
for once.

One Bud Heavy, Ramble

I placed a cigarette in my mouth and took a long, hopeless puff. I wasn't smoking to be cool. I was smoking for the dopamine. There wasn't a single soul around. Just a pigeon, looking like the same desperate shade of gray as the smoke. I thought, maybe this would eat away at me and only leave the debris. She was mad at me, again. I looked up at the sky, sitting down, back against the wall. In between puffs, I whispered, "Here's to good health and happy thoughts." Went back into the bar and spent the last of my bucks on a Budweiser. Sat alone listening to a band play "Sweet Caroline." There was nothing sweet about it. Everyone was smiling and dancing and all I could think about was another cigarette and wondering who covers a sing-along song. It is so hard to stay in the moment when you are such a cynic. Kurt Cobain and I are the same; not easily amused. I walked home that star-tangled night in the name of good health.

Two Truths and a Lie

I ate eggs this morning,
kicked a bad habit,
and said goodbye to my lover.

Wrote a song about a lonely town,
drove to Brooklyn with the windows down,
I'm happy now.

Two truths and a lie,
driving 'til I figure out my life.

I left the map at home,
my pockets full of change,
there is a piñata in the backseat of this '83 Chevrolet.

Nothing has changed,
I have a beard now,
renting a room downtown.

Two truths, a lie,
driving 'til I figure out this life.
Two truths and a lie.

Thought, after thought, after thought.
I miss her,
she misses me.

The truth will remain at the bottom of the sea,
along with the piñata and Chevy.
My only friend,
the amiable sea.

Jack

My eyelids, they ache,
for my soul,
does not know,
how I was not born with the Beatniks
as I savor the same wine,
you indulged.

Roll Tide

I stared at the stars
and shot my gun at the moon
that night in Alabama
when it all came unglued.

Roll tide, roll tide,
roll.

I wrote a letter to my uncle
and placed it under the doormat.
Retraced my steps to the place
that meant the most to me.

Roll tide, roll tide,
roll.

Read lines from William S. Burroughs' "Junkie,"
sang some sad, sad songs next to fire rings,
jumped tracks in my mind
and spun a top wishing I would die.

Roll tide, roll tide,
roll.

Seeking a town with less talk,
a town with more rock 'n' roll.
I spoke so much those days,
and thought even more.

I watch the sunrise every morning now,
and take consideration to the kids' questions.

As I collect the news from the hobo
on the corner I whisper 'bama's mantra:

Roll tide, roll tide,
roll.

My Grandpa, A Goddamn Sailor

Fun time rhymes,
glance to the sea,
a ship named *Tabernacle*
will return to me.

Sun-stroked captain,
a poem never told,
tuna on toast
gave him a heart of gold.

Beard curtained lips
and a slur of words,
tattoo on his arm
of ink soaked sparrow birds.

"Smoke this pipe, son,"
he told me.
"Fill it up with Celtic tea.
Take one sip,
travel the seven seas.
Son,
find a lover.
One who honors your idols,
and love her,
even if you must travel,
overseas."

Magic Moths

Take me somewhere else,
where I can see the grass grow
without feeling jittery
because everyone here is so witty.
I would love to be able to see, breathe, and believe
that nature will save me,
but my job is in the city,
yours is overseas.

So,
I started sailing.

Moons like dandelions,
and the stars, oh the stars,
the kindest magic moths
circling around our awakened heads
just like crowns and halos.
It will be royalty;
it will be peace.

Set sail to this place,
overseas.

Halving Wishbones

Searching for seashells
in abandoned alleys.
Halving a wishbone with my own two hands.
My mind keeps splitting like rock to sand,
but the more I meditate,
it's like whitewash resting on land.

My thoughts were grim.
Yes, my thoughts were full of fear.
But now, my friend, I understand,
now, I'll be the one to help you see clear.

Bring a canteen,
a can of beans,
a grin and some whiskey.
We will head for Big Sur, the sea,
the desert, and Joshua Tree.

Just us,
talking amongst the stars,
camping with coyotes,
until we can be understood.
No interruptions.
No need for recognition.

Two souls skipping stones,
two souls halving wishbones.

The Balloon and the Bodhisattva

A circle of kids surrounds me
hand in hand chanting around me.
Asking obscure and obtuse questions.
Like, why do you have freckles and red hair?
Do you want to play truth or dare?
Where do we go when we die?
You're 25, you should know,
right?

I stand up and squeeze between Ned and Nancy,
clammy hand in clammy hand.
I begin to sing a soft,
sweet melody.
We stomp our feet,
clap our hands,
and forget about answering the serious questions,
yet again.

The kids mean well,
and ask valid questions.
Like, who is God? Is he like the Buddha?
Does he float on his back and let the breakers bring
him ashore?
Or is God dead?

There is an air of honesty,
a sincere silence the kids can sense
radiating from my unclear consciousness.

Then Ned pipes up,

"It will all be okay, in the end.
Let's just sing and dance until then.
We're like balloons,
the way we are all different colors,
and the way we can be here one day
and then float off just like magic.
Did you know that?
When you let go of a balloon it just goes up and up
and up,
like magic.
It never pops!
Past the birds, the redwoods, the clouds, the moons,
and even God.
Balloons are angels.
That's what I think.
One day we will all be balloons.
One day,
my feet won't touch the ground,
and I will be magic."

Nice Day

The weather looks nice
when I look to the south,
past your eyelids,
past your mouth.

The breakers roll in,
fog rolls out.
The pigeons coo,
humans chop wood.

All the sage and rosemary
collected by calloused hands,
placed in half-full tin teacups
of the freshest streams.

Breathing is slow,
thoughts are clear
in the cabin.
Kindness is abundant,
food is scarce.

We sit and speak
profound things.
Like Zen Buddhism,
gentrification,
barber shops in Australia's West End,
sins.

We end each night under a warm wool rug,
with a simple prayer
for all sentient beings.

Thumb Up

Smell the roses for me today.
Eat well and smile a bit more than usual.
Tap your toes to the sound of the blues.
Think about the cosmos once, maybe twice.

Choose the high road.
Give a big thumb up to an old guy.
Truly live it up.
A cappella with the sound of your
shuffling feet/heartbeat,
for God's sake,
it's all about the simple things.

There is a sign to the left that reads, *Take Your Time*.
A sign to the right that says, *It's About Damn Time*.
Arm your eyes with those wayfarers.
Knock down the walls.
Hold my old soul as we head for the hills.

The sunrise is waiting for us.

I Am the Universe

My eyelids,
the petals.

My pupils,
the universe.

All talk is nonsense.
Chaos and commotion,
I suddenly lose balance
until I realize I am the universe.

The Milky Way on my knees
and the heart of the constellation rising from the seas.
I am transparent when I catch the disease.
Before it cuts me free.

Pest Like a Pisces

David Attenborough called me a pest,
so now all I do is hide in my nest.
Holding my breath,
CO_2 is all I have left.

Lake Placid

It's the honey on the doorknob.
House keys lost in the West Indies.
Indian food gone wrong,
kinda day.

Water balloon to the face.
Hand to the burner.
Tears on toes,
kinda day.

Even the sea seems sad.
The grass dull.
Cereal stale.
My face pale.

So I sold my soul.
Put a rucksack on a pole.
Took a walk today,
to a lake not far away.

Kicking dust and humming jazz.
One step, two step, by three
I am free.
Free of the muddled puddles of the mind.
The fog stricken conundrum I call time.

Sitting Indian-style
on a Mexican rug.
Amongst the birds and the ferns,
a fire burns.

No wildfire or brushfire,
but a self-contained peaceful pyre.

Take a break and hum your way to the lake.
I'll sit by the fire with you.

Bloody Nose

I have antibiotics in my blood,
fighting a lymph node in my neck.
Black coffee in my mug,
lifting me out of bed.
I still breathe through my nose.
I think I see red.
Yes, I see red.

Untitled

Branches like arms,
sap like blood.

I shake the leaf's hand,
it crumbles in my palm.

Falls to the ground,
to the grass,
to the ant's
playground.

Dad Bod

Everyone is too cool for me these days.
I'm in between adolescence and dad days.

Face hair like Hemingway,
denim jackets, smoking darts.

While I rock a straw hat paired with slacks
admiring the lines on a Honda Civic.

Beat

Please be kind with your words when I'm around.

No gossip or negative nonsense;
I'd rather sit in silence
with a cup of tea, the dog, and just read
about a log cabin in the snow, oh the life that would
be.

People would say, "But aren't you lonely?"
and I would say, "Kerouac, Snyder,
please explain."

An Autumn Walk

It's the cedar wood, it's the driftwood.
It's your oval eyes and your corduroys.
The sound of rain, a sunny day.
Give me the rolling tide, the rolling tide.

It's the autumn air, your bleach-blonde hair.
It's the sandy scene on the movie screen.
Give me your hand love, give me your hand.

It's the leaf you found, in that college town.
It's your favorite sweater, it's the autumn weather.
The barking beagle, the blazing fire.
Give me a love letter, give me your love.

Natural Beauty

Please take a deep breath,
wrap your arms around me,
for I am living, much like thee.
I will help with your worries,
if you let me.
Just sit awhile,
and listen to the leaves.

Joshua Tree

You saw me, atop that hill,
arms reach away from the sun.

I felt low, I felt so alone.
Remember? I could barely speak,
let alone stand.

So, I wrote;
soulful sonnets,
words of dust,
stanzas of stars.

Things can be so deceiving when you are running
from the moon.

At 7 a.m.,
you told me to head to Joshua Tree.
Where they stand like long-necked companions,
waiting for a handshake,
waiting for a hug.

At 8 a.m.,
I went.
Slept next to an old desert garden of yuccas,
and I read
my poems to them.

Most important, they shared some of their own,
in the whistle-breeze heat of summer.
I listened with my entire body.

From my toes to the toothpick dangling in my teeth,
I listened.

I came back with so many stories.
I came back with embers seared in my bones.
I came back with modesty in my breath.

Desert taught me how to stay sane in solitude.
Desert taught me you never,
travel alone.

I Know My Mailman Well

I wrote you a letter in the month of May.
You wrote back in June.
We decided to put them together and add a refrain.
We now live together and sing in harmony,
nearly every day.

Apocalypse

I'll walk to the end of the world with you.
To the place where the orchestra plays the outro
to nearly seven billion singing seats.
We will share the last apple ever shared on earth;
the Adam and Eve of the afterlife.

All the streetlights will go red,
when the last song ends.
And there will be a sea of trees
just sitting, staring, sifting
through their unwritten scroll.
Reclining their chairs
and waiting for the last page to be read.
But not us, my friend.
Oh no, not us.
We stand tall and unwavering.
Like the redwoods, like the child who just turned
three, like the song turned up with the windows down
when we turned sixteen.

But then you will anxiously say to me,
"Pelly, my faith is weak,
we've discussed religion
and it's all still so Greek to me."

In a nervous, yet confident tick of the tongue
I reply with this, some sort of fabled riddle that will
give you life again:
"God is in the dust, the cosmos, and Saturn's rings.
God is in my bones, my nose, and every breath I
breathe.

God is the heart of the sun, as the night sky comes to
life.
God is a metaphor, God is a mime.
God is just a word,
so let's be God for this one night."

As we clutch our lucky pennies,
and kiss the crowd farewell
we jump into the water of the infinite abyss's well.

Saddled atop the stars we were born from
we graffiti the night sky.
We live and die,
one last time.

This is all a script for what has not played out yet.
But please, promise me this.
Promise me, you will guide me.
Promise me, you will be the one who plays double
Dutch with me when the world ends.
Promise me, you will wipe the tears from my face
when the last words are said.
And lastly,
promise me;
we will run like the bull and fly like the bird,
hold each other's hand,
and welcome all that are scared.

After the outro,
I will sit by the fire with you.

In the debris,
we'll heat our tea.

Tea in the Woods

Tea in the woods,
tea in the woods,
tea in the woods.

A mantra I chant each morning.
Honey atop a chamomile petal,
ebbing and flowing.
A snowflake relinquished in a river;
every sip,
a modest sonnet in my mind.

Sign Language

I place my finger on your chest.
Figure eight around your breasts.
Place my palm on a beating song.
Feels like a ton of thoughts has been lifted off
the one I love.

Dear, the Coffee is Ready

She wore flannel to bed
and spoke in pun.
Sang about the good times at the top of her lungs.

She went from selling lemonade to selling drugs,
now she lays in a bed of dandelions
near the graveyard on Queens Road.

So Far from Death

I wrote more like a poet when I was seven.
Words so eloquent they put you in the moment.
A fish out of water, witnessing its first breath,
so far from death, oh so far from death.

It is Okay

I realized it is okay,
for the mosquito to bite me,
for old friends not to like me,
to call in sick on a rainy day.
I realized it is okay.

Oboe

The one escape this kid ever had was his oboe.
Locked doors, playing
along with phonograph records;
his meditation, temporary drug.
And everyone who ever loved him floated
around the room as musical notes.
So, he was never alone in his solitary confinement.
And on nights he played,
he would dream in colors.
So, he decided to play every night.

Now, growing old
he lived alone
with his oboe, a snow globe, a felt pen.
Wrote all his songs in the first person.
When he played his cardinal-colored instrument
he was in the moment.
What's more poetic than an oboe and an awakened
old man?

He would cry,
over the words he sang.
He couldn't recall the words the next day,
they just came like the wind, the rain, and the sun.

And these songs were only shared with the stars,
so there was no need to remember.
And every night, since he was a kid in his room,
he fell asleep to the sound of the oboe,
dreaming in color and flying with friends.

The snow globe's iridescent bubbles rained down.
His felt pen drew a giant blue jay
that whistled to the tune of his oboe,
and the words, oh the words,
were scriptures,
for the insane.
He sang in his sleep,
"This is the space where there is no pain."

It was the oboe that made him dream this way.

Words, Older Now

I own a green bike,
a wool hat,
and a vintage Scrabble piece.

Nothing more,
I'd rather have less.

I own a pebble from Texas,
a paintbrush,
and a hockey puck.

This is more
in my eyes.

I own a window,
an imagination,
and a sunray
that just swept me off my feet
and dropped me overseas.

You see,
if you look at life
as thunder and lightning
you'll be the first one to get stuck
in a pinhole time machine hell scene.
I've been there.

I've never been
very good with directions -
but you can't blame me with my head out the window

hootin' and hollerin'
at the gods before me
and the almighty gods to come -
maps are minute when I'm thinking of
the kids' questions.

But, I'm older now.
So, I know the song the sparrow sings.
The fact is the song isn't sung by the sparrow
but by the leaves in the trees.

I see in you
the stars and the moon.
This is more,
now that I'm
older now.

Knock 'em Dead

I put my beagle in my backpack,
covered up the Om patch
with a dollar bill
in the name of greed.
Stuck my thumb out over the hill,
and overseas.

My mom taught me,
"Put your best foot forward and knock 'em dead,
buckwheat."
You never know what is buried there unless you
dig around.
And mom,
I've been digging for hours,
I've been digging for answers.
On my,
meditation pad.
In my,
beginner's mind.

Grandma, The Pine in the Wind

The pine in the wind,
the scent of sin.
I knew your number by heart,
but the receptionist said true love was dead.
I turned into an introvert,
loathed time alone.
My subconscious flashed with demons,
luckily that changed with the seasons.
I wrote a letter to my grandmother,
thanking her,
for the positive-thought gene,
I finally found in me.

Mount Youth

The stars came out to play with the moon that day.
The ground beneath our feet
turned into an ice skating rink.
Our boots turned into blades
and the stakes of life were raised,
for that one day.

The stacks of Buddhist books in my brain,
could not bring me back from the past.
Reminiscing on that day,
nostalgia can be a beautiful thing.

I saw smiling faces of youth,
Eli, John, James,
Theo, Thalia, Sia.
All the kids from town were skiing
through frozen streams
with boots hanging around their necks
and they were all holding hands,
heading to Mount Youth.

It was after school and before dinner.
Happy hearts and empty stomachs.
Not a drip of drama.
Crisp cutting of grass underneath the falling of leaves.
We held hands. It was simple.
No need for hairstyles or fashion statements.
Boys wearing figure skates and
girls wearing hockey skates.

It was a feeling,
a great,
fragile feel.

Barnacles

I saw sunlight on my granddad's knuckles
when he reached 70,
maybe 80 miles per hour.

I was too young to understand the feeling,
but the genes fall close to the tree.

It wasn't long 'til I was backseat, barebones,
collecting barnacles off granddad's blooming body.
With the weight of the sea,
and Jack's eulogy,
in me.

I sailed on.

Sun Broke

The sun broke through the sonnet
 about the same time my voice turned shaky,
"I swear to God I'm trying so goddamn hard."
I keep saying to my idols.

And they keep saying to me,
"Remember your Levi's coat and that meditation pad,
 for the times get tougher."

Bixby Bridge

Skipping stones out to sea,
wondering where you'll be,
when I'll be brewing tea
on the Bixby Bridge.

You called me from a pay phone,
from what town I don't know,
and you said you'd meet me
on the Bixby Bridge.

We drank wine from the bottle,
made plans for tomorrow,
ate crackers with the Brie,
held hands 'til we were eighty.

But there's something wrong in this song,
it doesn't sound quite the same,
as when we swung our legs
off the Bixby Bridge.

Let's jump the tracks,
Never look back, never look back, never look back.

Let's hum along,
to this burning song, this burning song, this burning
song.

Let's take all these friends,
to a secret island, a secret island, a secret island.

I never want to leave this night.
Never want to leave your side.
This night,
your side.

Sage Travels, Pelly

Bury me neck deep in a garden of sage,
leave me nothing but my nose and God's grace.

Oh Dear

Rolling around in the mud,
not minding my jeans.
Sketching scenes of my teens
with my best friend, KT.

I had a bucket list full of phobias,
until I saw the deer run through the woods.
Our hands interlocked by the waterfall.
The herd, like me, dodging debris.

So we sat on moss,
swam in streams,
listened to a few of my favorite things:

"Loro" by Pinback,
"Peacock Tail" by Boards of Canada,
"A Word Aptly Spoken" by Ray Barbee.
Clearing my head for a moment of clarity,
when I turned 23.

Out of the Country

I'm out in the country.
Out wild and somewhat free.
I don't have to brush my teeth,
every day.
I sleep near the railroad tracks,
floss my teeth with rain.
Trade my name with men who fought in 'nam.
They have stories, unlike the soccer moms.

Out in the country.
Out wild and free.

Bless It All

God bless the teenage riots,
the meditation room in the millionaire's mansion,
the sunspots on my only grandfather's
soft-spoken skin,
for the waves of inspiration after a long, long lull.

God bless the corner of my room echoing acoustics,
the barefoot feet dancing a step offbeat,
my box of miscellaneous gifts,
from friends speaking different languages.

God bless the atheist, the bomb, the butterfly,
the float-on feeling after a fucking frantic
panic attack,
all the stars I've yet to see,
all the gangsters wishing they could travel overseas.

God bless the perfectionist
who keeps painting over his self-portrait,
and for love, love, and of course, all the above.

Wake of the Wildflower

I knew you were thinking of me,
and that is all that matters.
Your letter makes sense,
a lot like this fire lookout.
I made it to the top,
fell into a rabbit hole or two,
slapped on my chucks and a hard hat,
couldn't have made it without your walking stick.
Spring has sprung,
I am a sailor in the wake of the wildflower.
Hop aboard,
dear friend.
The westerlies will guide us,
together.

Yrs,
Pelly

P.S.
I am doing better, too.

Shout out to ///

Brie Verdugo, thanks for your pro copy-editing skills –
stay gold.
Road Dawgs, I owe you all a beer.
My American and Australian friends and family.
My editor/publisher, NS.
And KT <3.

**TIRED COAST
PUBLISHING ™**

tiredcoast.com
@tiredcoast

James Buffalo & A Fit Of Bad Dharma (2013)

Brands & BullS**t (2017)

for KT, from overseas (2018)

2 poems

by
Nigel James Schroeder

Road Dawg Blues Forever

Threw our worry-logs,
into the pavement flames,
origami birds in black smoke out the rear view of the
RV.
Got to get going,
got to get—
along.
Burning soul and rubber up the Tired Coast,
California's undercover loneliness lovers;
headlight angels.
Honked the horn at a gas station in Carpinteria,
Pelly hopped on in,
sat down next to me.
And somewhere outside Goleta,
I wrote a letter to God.
Said,
"Sorry for the hassle,
could you lasso these horses?
I can't run with them anymore."
Forgot to mail it,
read it to Pelly instead.
He didn't say anything,
still in our bodies,
I got to thinking that the apocalypse of things had
turned us into sea glass.
After a while,
some long silence,
waves crashing against rocky Gaviota shoreline, Pelly
says, "The best part about writing letters to God is
that you don't need a post office to mail them."

He thinks of KT,
looks out the window of the RV;
sea glass.
Stampless and alone,
I feel the curves of his of sorrow at 70 miles per hour,
Cott pushing this old rig,
as fast as she'll go.
Don't say anything for a while,
waves crashing,
sit and stare,
quite,
'til I think,
"The best part about the Road Dawg blues is the,
howling."
Pelly smiles and says,
"We can blame it on American television,
this sadness of ours,
the slow-cooked microwave dinner that is everything;
huddle around the TV set and make babies."
I reply,
"Blame it on the collective-*me*,"
and that's probably right enough;
for right now.
And near the San Simeon pier, Cott says,
as I sit in the pit,
"Focus on the wheels that spin on this here rig,
the view from the old cockpit,
that's it!"
And oh poor me,
here I am forgetting to mail my God letters,
screaming with my eyes out the windows of the RV—
"Make room for the howling!

Speak to me, ocean!
Love you my sweet suffering!
Does this thing have a shower?"
Pelly says,
"Cheer up Duck,
the high school kids that drove by Kerouac ride
through our town too."
Drunk on the Central Coast,
feet up by the fire,
I ask Cott,
"Is love a good smoke?
Is love a cloud in the sky?
Is love the seals on Gorda beach?"
Cott smiles,
shakes his head and says,
"Love is this sweet guitar of mine,
the licks it spits.
The radio cracking out in the old cockpit,
the Dawgs,
man."
The big conifers in Big Sur say,
"You'll be all right,
we think…"
Take their word for it,
'cause I ain't no philosopher,
no more.
The Dawgs will always take
another, when you're buying,
so at the tavern, I'll lay the plastic down the line every
time because I love these headlight angels.
Burn the map,
eat a poem,

kill a song.
Viking funeral, me in the cockpit,
light a fire in my soul and let it float like a lantern
above the Japanese friendship gardens.
Bless the Road Dawgs,
Road Dawg blues forever,
I tried,
to listen to what Pelly says,
to live forever,
long pavement;
love forever,
headlight angels.

Perigee Hearts

Must be the pull,
must be the moon,
must be you!